Close But Not Touching

ALSO BY JEAN SANDS

Gandy Dancing (Antrim House, 2009)

Close But Not Touching

Poems by

Jean Sands

Antrim House
Simsbury, Connecticut

Copyright © 2017 by John H. Sheedy

Except for short selections reprinted for purposes of
book review, all reproduction rights are reserved.
Requests for permission to replicate should
be addressed to the publisher.

Library of Congress Control Number: 2017947581

ISBN: 978-1-943826-36-0

First Edition, 2017

Printed & bound by Ingram, Inc.

Book design by Rennie McQuilkin

Front cover acrylic painting by Jean Sands

Inner title page photograph by Tom Kutz

Author photograph by Cortney Davis

Antrim House
860.217.0023
AntrimHouse@comcast.net
www.AntrimHouseBooks.com
21 Goodrich Road, Simsbury, CT 06070

This book is dedicated to Jean's brother,
Fred DeClement, keeper of the memories.

Acknowledgments

Grateful acknowledgment to the editors of the following publications in which these poems first appeared, at times in earlier versions:

Collinsville Writers' Collective: "Lillis Road"

Connecticut River Review: "Close But Not Touching"

H.O.W. Journal: "When Mother Stopped Remembering," "The Policeman Is Your Friend," "How a Relationship Dies," "Saving for Good"

Poetpourri: "Meeting My Ex at the County Fair," "After the Party"

If Jean Sands were here, she would certainly want to thank Cortney Davis, a longtime friend and fellow poet with whom she shared most of these poems and who has helped me organize them for this volume. Thanks also to Honor Moore, who mentored Jean in her formative years as a poet and continued to support her more mature poetry. I join Jean in thanking the members of the Shepaug River Writers for their insightful criticism; her Writers' Work workshop students for lending an attentive ear; her sons Ron, Dave, Steve and Matt; and editor/publisher Rennie McQuilkin for working with me on this manuscript.

– Jack Sheedy

Table of Contents

Foreword by Jeanne Bryner / ix

I.

When Mother Stopped Remembering / 4
What If? / 6
Becoming Helen / 7
Carrots / 10
Photos at the Cemetery / 12
Lillis Road / 14
The Peach Farmer's Daughter / 15
Pigs / 16
Plum / 17
The Music Lesson / 18
Danbury Fair / 19

II.

Turn That Goddamn Thing Down / 22
Four Sons / 24
First Visit, Boston 1989 / 25
Night Sounds / 26
Suicide / 27
Swimmer / 28
The Policeman Is Your Friend / 29
Father Poem / 30
Summer Heat / 31
Not Another Gulf War / 32
Coward / 34
Summer Camp / 36

III.

Car Ride / 38
Leaving Home / 40
How a Relationship Dies / 41
Pink Carnations / 42
What If He Wakes? / 43
Close But Not Touching / 45
Divorce Settlement / 46
Working in a Discount Store after the Divorce / 47
Saving the Universe / 48
Cleaning Her House / 49
Collection Day / 51
Birds / 52
After the Party / 53

IV.

Meeting My Ex at the County Fair / 56
Christmas in New York / 57
What Hunger Does / 59
Rain / 60
Far from Home / 61
Baking Cookies / 63
As Evening Comes / 64
At the Vet's Office / 65
Poem for a Friend with M.S. / 67
Beautiful / 68
Saving for Good / 69

Afterword by Jack Sheedy / 71

About the Author / 73

Foreword

In Gregory Orr's book, *Poetry as Survival*, he tells us, *One of a story's primary purposes is to lay claim to experience. Autobiographical storytelling can take personal experience back from silence, shame, fear, or oblivion. It says, "I cherish this," or "This haunts me."* Jean Sands' book of narrative poems reclaims parts of her life story and gives her experiences, some nearly unspeakable, a shape in the language of poetry.

Like poets through the ages, Sands wonders about geography and her place in this world, how her life might have been better, could certainly have been worse. Displaced from her family after various abuses, it's a wonder her pen found its way to the page. Here is Dickinson's call for *letting go* after *great pain*. The natural world of peaches and plums—sweet fruits desired, mouthed, and consumed—serve as a metaphor for the girl she was. It's with great empathy she speaks for those who are traumatized and must seek ways to repair themselves.

Through the lens of memory, Sands shows us the wheel of her life as a daughter, wife, homemaker, employee, and grandmother. We sense her hunger and her frustrations. Dressed as anger, sexuality, or disappointments, fire is ever present in her poems, and sometimes the flame is self-directed. We feel the poet receiving dents and bruises from partner choices and being tossed out of her marriages—but line by line, she reaches for help and continues to rise. Mother of four sons, she suffers a mother's heart and speaks honestly about war and politics and never really wanting a girl child. No doubt, her childhood experiences shaped this mindset.

The pages of our lives are constantly turning. And Sands acknowledges this by recording her own life with all its warts and roses in poetry. She does not shy away from lives braided to her own. She writes poetry for a dying friend with MS, her sick cat, her veterinarian, her ex-husbands, and takes us to the graves of her family. *It's all good,* she seems to be saying, *I have lived, loved, made mistakes and questioned the world around me. One day, I will die, and that's all right.*

There's a great capacity of forgiveness in this poet. We see it when she breaks off huge bouquets of lilacs for her mother and in the gentle scene at St. Patrick's in New York when her new, kind husband turns her face away from the homeless man dressed in the past. She is fully present at the table of her life and walks in communion with what has been and what will be. We must be grateful to such a woman for taking time to hang her poems on the line where all the neighbors can count the patches in her quilt.

– Jeanne Bryner, poet, fiction writer, playwright

What is to give light must endure burning.

– Viktor Frankl

At the Centre is a door
that does not open
but can be entered
when the right word is spoken.

– Adam Wyeth (from "Aspen")

CLOSE
BUT NOT TOUCHING

I.

When Mother Stopped Remembering

She called everything "the thing."

*Get me that thing in the closet to sweep the floor
the thing to scrub the pot*

Last night at dinner with friends
I couldn't remember the word *memorial*—
there is a memorial in Warsaw,
a temple in Krakow, in Auschwitz,
a place where time stopped, the earth
split open and swallowed memories.

Seated at the restaurant's round table—
a journalist, a doctor, two poets, an abstract artist
who could hide a thousand souls in her paintings
but instead volunteers for the Shoah project.

We talk religion, each naming the one true way—
Catholic, Protestant, Judaism, the Universe.
We discuss art exhibits, colors brilliant
and shocking as a staring dead eye.

Mother couldn't name kitchen utensils
she'd used for forty years
but never forgot the German soldier
when she was a child in Hungary.

The journalist writes about rights,
marriages "the church" won't sanctify.
On weekends, the doctor photographs

blue sky, blood-red flowers, ivy
like fingers scratching Birkenau's walls.

At the table we talk about the mercy of God,
His benevolence to those who are good.
Where was God on Kristallnacht?
Was He at Auschwitz? Birkenau? Belzec?
Dachau? Treblinka? Buchenwald? Bergen-Belsen?

As Mother's memory failed she grew silent.
Her eyes clouded over. She gave up books.
In Germany, they emptied the shelves,
burned the books, the men, the women, the children.

What If?

I had been born in Austria or Hungary
like my mother's people instead of America.
What if my hair wasn't blond enough,
if my eyes weren't blue.
I could have been a 1940s orphan,
not even a distant cousin to call my own.
What if America was Kosovo and I was Albanian.
Would I be hustled to some backroom,
raped in the village square, beaten,
left in the gutter with a bullet in my head?
I could be living in El Salvador, Korea,
Darfur, Croatia, Colombia, Cuba.
I could have been the young man defiant
in Tiananmen Square,
the girl on fire in Vietnam.
The world grows smaller and still the murders go on
at the hands of the righteous,
the dictator, the bully
in Afghanistan, Indonesia, Zimbabwe,
Turkey, Pakistan, Palestine,
India, Nigeria, Russia, Rwanda, Chile,
Haiti, Israel, Iran, Iraq,
and as in Hitler's Germany
nobody stops them.

Becoming Helen

As I stand at the stove turning bacon
an old house comes to mind, so dilapidated and dirty

that in the end the only sensible renovation was destruction.
Windows rattled under my cloth as I scrubbed

while a man cranky with age lugged heavy storm windows
down a rickety ladder. I worried he would fall,

he worried a window would drop on me—
I was twenty-nine, divorced, helping out an old couple

for two dollars an hour to feed my three small boys.
Alex cursed the weight of ladders, snapped

at me for tossing paper towels in the garbage can
and not the fire barrel he lit once a week

but I forgave him, he was ninety, generous, sent me home
with fresh fish he caught, chicken, hamburger, steak.

He missed his brilliant career, the smell of a courtroom,
clients he defended. Sometimes he growled

at the miniature collie yipping at his heels.
He kenneled dogs, caged them in the cellar, swore

at their noise, the smelly newspapers damp with urine
he burned in a barrel behind a shed, its faded red roof

sloped to the ground. Grease splattered the chipped-enamel
stove I hated cleaning—remnants of fried bacon, horsemeat boiled

in ten-quart pots for the dogs he fed by hand.
Alex ate eggs off a bone china plate, held bacon

between his fingers for his collie, followed the stock market
like a hound running trails, growled at me *buy low, sell high*

as if I had the money.
In the bedroom his wife Helen bent over a beat-up typewriter,

wrote features for the Sunday Post, the straps
of a faded pink silk slip and a pilled blue sweater

draping her arthritic shoulders. She interviewed local celebrities,
cradled the phone under her chin while she typed.

Helen was seventy-five, sharp; I admired the way she worked
despite the weight of pain, a Parliament scorching her ashtray.

Occasionally she ventured out in a faded beige Pontiac,
a diabetic wearing a veiled hat, dated dress,

nicotine-stained white gloves grasping the wheel.
Sometimes we worked side by side, me dusting, her writing,

both of us deep in thought,
the lines of unborn poems zigzagging in my head as my cloth

moved back and forth across an ancient dresser, a table laden with junk.
Once she lived in Singapore, Bangkok, Paris, Chicago.

She quarreled with Capone, dined with an emperor,
lost a husband to malaria in China, an infant to typhoid in Tokyo.

I brought in her mail, thick manila envelopes bulging
with leads, she tore them open like a dog devouring bone.

Sometimes Alex torched her papers in the barrel, howled
like a hound, drove to the sleaziest bar in town.

Helen dyed her hair red, leaned over a pan while I poured
tepid water over pallid strands. Some days, cheeks rouged, gold broach

pinned to her breast, henna hair tucked under a hat,
we lunched with the mayor in the best restaurant in town,

Helen holding court like a queen whispering
a little powder, a little paint, makes a girl what she ain't.

Forty years later the keyboard clicks under my fingers,
unseen hands hover above mine.

Carrots

I'm out on the deck peeling carrots
where I always peel vegetables,
letting the papery orange fly from my scraper
onto the grass and I think of my mother cooking
on her Tappan range in the house my father built.
Cut carrots in two for beef stew,
into chunks for chicken soup
she said, teaching me her way.

The day is damp, chilly, mid September,
the sun sliding from clouds only on whim.
I look for a butterfly in the lilac bush
that leans over the rail
because after Mother died she came to me
as a yellow swallowtail and hovered around me,
landed on my hand. Ever since,
butterflies visit each summer,
rest in the lilacs, open,
offer their beauty, their trust.

Mother loved the lilac's sweet scent
and kept in her misty-green vase
the bunches I brought home,
cut from a country lot, vacant
but for the ruined rim of an old foundation.
My friend Lorraine and I made up stories—
a family that lived there in the 1930s,
went bust in the Depression,
a daughter our age sent to relatives,
the parents getting jobs with a circus
or died of heartbreak, buried

in the cemetery up the road,
how the house went to rot.
We never felt guilty cutting armloads
of purple for our mothers
from their gangly overgrown bushes.

There are no butterflies on this mostly gray day
and so I say into the stiff wooden air
Where are you, Mom?
and carry the carrots into the house,
cut them in chunks, drop them into
my simmering soup.

Photos at the Cemetery

First stop, my father's grave.
Mother lays flowers on stone
brother snaps a Polaroid—
the polished gray granite
Dad's name, Mother's name.

Next stop, Fairfield.
Mother's parents side by side
in that quiet wide lawn
where they lay since that 1940 night they died.
When she leans
against the stone, my brother
snaps a picture.

Once Father trimmed shrubs
on either side of the stone.
Mother pinched back red geraniums.
Weary now, she sits in the maroon Chevy
head resting against the passenger window.

Brother drives the Post Road
past a string of Burger Kings,
7-Elevens, Pizza Huts, glitzy neon signs.
Clouds move in above Norwalk
as brother circles a graveled drive,
stops near hay weed and marsh,
snaps a photo of grandfather's name
carved in worn red granite.

Father's favorite uncle Paulo
sleeps nearby, his wife Mary at his side.

Brother raises the camera
snaps the photo.

We head home where photos
line the shelves,
our ancestors in their best clothes,
squinting in the sun.

Lillis Road

At the end of a dirt road, iron gates —
the kind I searched for last summer,
a photo for a book I'm writing about creativity,
how it gets locked out, what lets it in.
The scrolled gates are spoiled by a No Trespassing sign,
a warning about dogs protecting sculptures,
perennials a gardener tends,
a terrace surrounded by marble gods,
Apollo, Aphrodite, Demeter, and Persephone
rising from Zeus's lair, a house made of stone
and white clapboard, a sun porch wider than the total space
of all three houses I've owned.
Just down the road, pre-fabs, a trailer
hanging crazy on the edge of a hill,
a yard full of noisy kids, cars left to rust, junk.
I remember the months driving back roads,
words hitting walls in my head, poems
refusing to form, and now on an early spring day,
sun pinned to a bright blue sky, daffodils dressing fields,
lime-colored leaves just opening their hands,
words flowing like lilac nectar,
I discover these gates intended to keep me out.

The Peach Farmer's Daughter

When her father died she laughed
knowing his hands couldn't touch her anymore
though years had passed since she'd spent time
in his company. Her mother saw to that,
sending her to a maiden aunt who couldn't keep her
from back seats, rushed her into an early marriage.

When his ashes arrived, the canister lay beside her,
sliding across the leather seat as easily as she did
on sexy summer nights. Driving the narrow rows
between the peach trees that hid her secrets,
she pressed the accelerator to the floor,
held the blue canister out the window,
let his ashes blow across the orchard.
When it was done, she parked at the end of a dirt road
wrestling memories—his liquor breath, his fingers inside.
She hated the farm, hated her father, the peaches,
the baskets, the barn, the doorway where she'd stand swaying.
She could still hear him saying, *Hula for me honey.*
Her mother divorced him but it was too late.
The daughter's marriages failed, she took lovers,
betrayed her family, her friends, her children.
And no matter how hard she tried to stand still
her hips kept moving,
keeping time to that old familiar metronome.

Pigs

Winter was hard
the barn eighty yards up hill
the boys lugging brook water
pails of scraps on the back porch
a pot of peels boiling on the stove
feed for an untimely litter
the stench of pig dung
clinging to leather boots
left on the grate to dry.
At butcher time, the hogs ran to the feed bucket,
ran to slaughter
the gun already cocked dropping them
beside their faithful farmer.

Plum

So young she doesn't believe
she could be split in half like a plum.

She doesn't know the farmer's hands
are rough from years working orchards

doesn't believe he'd take a bite
and toss her away.

The Music Lesson

My bow coaxing Hungarian Dance No. 5
from my violin's strings. Next to the piano,
arms folded across his chest,
Leroy Anderson watches and listens.
His daughter and I take violin lessons
from a man who could make a Stradivarius sing.
For weeks Mr. Jones coached me
encouraging my best performance
proud that his protégé played so well.
He wanted to show me off but that Saturday morning
I forgot my music book, the arrangement
I knew how to play left home on the dresser
next to my pink radio, a pink piggy bank
that rattled when I shook it. When I put my bow
to the string the notes were scratchy and thin.
I was just a kid, ten or eleven years old.
I didn't know that Leroy Anderson
was a famous composer. But I remember
my teacher, the way his face fell
in disappointment.

Danbury Fair

It was October and I was running counters
in a food booth at the Danbury Fair—
hotdogs, sauerkraut, burgers,
grinders with sausage, peppers and onions,
hot greasy fries, chicken halves.

There were two guys on the grill
Phil and Al, up from Florida,
both with smiles that could melt ice.
One a sharp dresser, the other in dirty whites,
Phil peeling potatoes and onions, chopping
them with peppers all day long,
wiping those huge hands I longed to have touch me.

The air at the fairgrounds smelled of beer,
sausage, pepper and onions. Back then,
I was always hungry.

II.

Turn That Goddamn Thing Down

for Ron

Me at the bottom of the stairs shouting
Turn that goddamn thing down!
Zeppelin screaming from my boys' room
where they strum air guitars, drown me out.

It is 1980 and soon they will graduate
from high school. I am a naive mother,
have no idea they will travel far from me—
the oldest joining a carnival, his brother
in the Navy. The day I drop the sailor off
at the recruitment center, long blond curly hair
down his back, I have no idea
I won't see him for four years.

The carnival kid comes home
every few weeks, stays a few days,
eats, showers, washes dirty clothes
he brings in a huge, black-plastic
garbage bag slung over his shoulder. I hate
him working with a carnival, afraid
some seedy character running a ride
or working a chisel game on the midway
will hurt him.

My shrink friend says kids have to break hard
or they won't be able to leave home,
that separating from parents is natural,
a part of growing up.
That's really what all the arguments were about—

trying to dislike each other so the separation would be
easy, not about the loud music
I would one day miss. They had to leave
and I had to let them go
though God knows none of it was easy.
I couldn't stop crying after they moved out
and thirty years later, when I hear
Babe I'm Gonna Leave You
playing on the radio,
I don't turn it down.

Four Sons

No daughters please.
That's what I begged the gods
each time I was pregnant.

I don't have patience for girls, I said,
messing around my kitchen,
wanting attention, bitching through PMS.

But now, my sons are grown and have wives—
and on holidays my place is the last place
they want to be. Girls go home to their mothers.
A son is a son till he takes a wife,
but his mother will love him all of her life.

First Visit, Boston 1989

for Steven

Your apartment is four flights up
from a bottle-littered alley.
A blue ten-speed bike is chained to the stair rail.
There are two locks on your door,
solid oak an axe can break through.
The ceilings are high, peeling
dingy white paint. The Venetian blinds
let in streaks of light. The waterbed leaks.
In the sink, dishes coated with spaghetti sauce,
the tap water tastes of chlorine,
the toilet is temperamental.
On every wall posters of rock stars
juxtaposed against the yellow tulips
blooming all over town.
Brownstones and brick walls
butt up against each other here.
On Beacon Hill
kids run out nursery school doors
into their fathers' arms,
the BMWs parked at the curb.
On every wide sill, books,
lamps, orchids.
When I head for home
I leave money on your dresser.

Night Sounds

for Matt

The night my son comes home upset
after seeing his father
for the first time in a year,
an animal screams
outside the bedroom window.
My new husband walks the road
in his pajamas only to discover
sound carries greater distance in dark
and the animal, taunted by a predator
or caught in a trap, is deep in the woods
behind the house of a neighbor
too sound asleep or uncaring
to turn on the light.

In sleep, my son bangs into walls,
the animal's scream and his father's voice
tangle. He dreams they are hunting again,
the one time he was forced to go,
the rifle pointed toward the sky, the pheasant
falling, the dog's triumphant retrieval,
the bird's last gurgle, then the muskrat trapped
for its pelt, his father ripping the clamp
from its foot, the animal still crying
when its head hit the rock.
For a second my son stops breathing
then struggles from sleep, escaping
the suffocating sheets,
the pain of something dying.

Suicide

The clothes line full from porch to pole
pulled too tight snapped

covering the ground with shirts,
underwear, everything in the last load.

The blue shirt you wore that day in the car
when you said "pills" for the first time

is dirty. My heart stopped dead
in my chest, my ears pounded

and by the time I had my breath
the car was off the road.

You said pills cure pain and I panicked
phoned doctors, psychiatrists,

did everything to save you.
It was months before you'd mount

the new bike you found in the kitchen
the morning your father left

months before you raced
that Schwinn against wind.

Swimmer

When our son broke his wrist
in the middle of the night,
it took one frantic hour
from the time some doctor woke me
to race thirty miles of back roads.
Earlier that day I left him at camp,
a boy in red bathing trunks
twirling a towel like a lariat,
running with a gang down to the water.

Near the cabins, where the volleyball net
hooks to the mess hall, a row of mothers
waved goodbye while I imagined children
limp as pond weed pulled from water.
Fearing the worst, I never dreamed
he would fall from the top bunk.

That night, I expected you to be there,
holding our child's hand. Instead,
one pale boy lay against white sheets
watching for you, his perfect blue eyes
full of pain, his shattered wrist wrapped in bandage.
The next day, my sturdy swimmer
home on the couch, swallowed aspirin
and dreamed of water, the way it slips
through a boy's fist.

The Policeman Is Your Friend

is what they said when I was a kid
but when the cop in California
was video-taped beating a motorist,
I remembered the night a cop
slammed my son up against a car
for *questioning,* then reached over
and cracked his friend's nose
with a billy club.
The cop said they were drunk
but the truth about that night is
rain had just left its last drops on the road,
four nineteen-year-old boys
headed for the rock music exploding
from a roadhouse door.
None of them were drunk.
One burnt tail light was enough
to pull them over. The cop smiled
and cuffed the kid who stepped between.
It was nineteen eighty-one,
and camcorders were just coming into their own.

Father Poem

You wonder why your son barely speaks to you
why he keeps your grandson from you.

If I said I told you this would happen
if you left us, you would say I turned him
against you and never remember the nights
he watched at the window for you
to pick him up for the weekly visit.

Instead you chose to spend your time
with women and left him waiting,
sallow-faced and sad. Those nights
he sobbed into his pillow believing
I couldn't hear.

Some nights he stood at that window
twisting his hands, thinking you were just late,
not knowing you were in Colorado or Kansas
but hadn't told him. Sometimes
the phone rang half an hour past pick up time
and, embarrassed at being forgotten,
he ran into his room and closed the door.

There were the phone calls you never made
the birthday gifts you never bought
the good times the two of you never had—
and now, when he has a son of his own
you wonder why he doesn't speak to you
why he doesn't want you around.

Summer Heat

for David

It was a prank really,
kids bored by summer heat
tossing matches they never thought
could burn eighteen acres of woods.
My son vanished escaping the blaze
leaving a black scar in all that loveliness,
ran from the beating waiting for him
in the big red barn.

A search party formed—
neighbors with CB radios,
bikers with long hair, off-duty cops,
parents with kids of their own who just might do
such a foolish thing. Paramedics with oxygen
and needles, hunters with dogs, teenagers
who knew him, and men who took the day off
formed a human chain that moved
across the valley. In the barn
his stepfather refused to search, instead
turned to his work igniting acetylene,
his hands the torch he used to burn everything.

Not Another Gulf War

I don't want my boys beat up
at the hands of the president
or anyone else
with the authority
to send them into danger.
I mean War. WAR!
What a big word. What
small men use it. War
is what kills the soul.
War is what kills the body,
sends boys home in bags
for their mothers to bury.
War. I don't want my boys
anywhere near it.
I don't want them part
of that dirty business.
And I'm helpless.
Mothers don't count here,
or in Iraq where they hold arms high,
afraid bombs will fall
and kill their children,
where anthrax slips through masks,
and friendly fire kills.
I remember Vietnam.
How safe I felt
my little boys sitting on the carpet
in front of the TV drinking hot chocolate
eating just-baked cookies
and watching Bugs Bunny.
I can still hear them laugh.
Oh we were snug in our small house then.

When my boys grew up,
one joined the Navy
and spent twenty-nine years
on foreign shores
and I haven't stopped praying,
haven't stopped wishing
he were home.
Safe.

Coward

Vanity asks the question, "Is it Popular?" Conscience asks the question, "Is it right?" And there comes a time when one must take a position that is neither safe, not politic, nor popular, but one must take it because one's conscience tells one that it is right.

Martin Luther King, Jr.

Listen Mister Realist,
black and white conservative,
you call me coward
when I turn away from pictures
of swollen-bellied children
whose bones protrude
right through sleep
into dreams that turn night
into holocaust.
I see dying
in their hungry eyes
and they haunt me.

No Mister-that's-the-facts,
I don't watch Safer or Stahl
dig deep into a history that brings
Rwanda and Darfur to their knees.
Go ahead, call me coward
but the truth is I can't change the world
by wishing, and twenty dollars
to Save the Children
barely feeds one for a week.

I cover my eyes while you nod,
safe in your armchair review, say

that's the way it is
underdeveloped nations
uneducated masses
safe distance from us.

Go ahead, call me a coward
for not watching.
What makes you feel safe
scares hell out of me.

Summer Camp

On the first nice day after a week
of rain, my youngest son comes home from camp,
face bruised from pillow fights

the counselors couldn't stop, the cabins
and heat, a hundred screaming kids
cooped like chickens.

The boy has a bruise above his nose,
a scratch on his left temple,
a spot like a ruined plum on his thigh.

His glasses are broken and he's still wearing
the same green shirt. When I left him at camp
loons were calling across the water.

Nights, while I lay awake worrying
his weak wrist would snap
he played ping pong, Parcheesi.

While I thought of rain—
was he wet? was he cold?
he was, at last, happy as the loon
singing, singing in the night.

III.

Car Ride

The last time I got out of a car so fast it was winter.
I opened the door and practically jumped
into six inches of snow falling
in flakes thick enough to blind any driver
no matter how fast the wipers swiped.
Never mind that my husband was drunk,
veered all over the road, on purpose,
aimed for an embankment, threatened
to kill me because I begged
Slow down, stop the car, let me out!

When the car jolted to a halt I escaped, refused
to get back in although we were a mile from home
where our babies slept in their beds, refused,
though I wore high heels and knew
I couldn't walk that distance in snow
on that terrible night in that terrible storm
and stood beside the Plymouth wagon
shivering in my black cocktail dress
until he handed me the keys.
I slid behind the wheel, gunned the gas,
the tires spinning us back onto the road.
I crawled the car all the way home,
him raging and cursing on the seat beside me.

Last night when I stepped from our car it was different—
though fright had been building with every jerk
of the wheel. Up and down the busy city street
you read gold numbers on glass doors searching
for 605. You turned in and out of store parking lots,
bumped over curbs, drove so fast behind cement block buildings
cars came at us head on.

No, it wasn't the same as that night in the snow,
still I had to escape,
had a burning need just to walk away.
I tried to stifle the words in my head—
I can't do this anymore, I can't do this anymore—
but desperation overtook me as you circled

and swerved searching for the place
where poetry was about to begin,
refused to ask directions of the couple
holding hands on the curb, of anyone
who might end the tension rising between us.

Suddenly, I couldn't take it any more
opened the car door at a red light, slammed it shut,
walked one block after another until I caught up
with the couple who pointed to the café.

I swear I didn't plan to get out of the car
but visions of my door rammed and dented
flared up, and just like that night in the snow
words pounding in my head.

I can't do this anymore,

I can't do this,

I can't.

Leaving Home

When they said I had to leave my home
stars shot off in the sky like meteors
falling into space's black hole.

There was this comic book when I was a kid,
Captain Thunder or something like that,
the son watching for his astronaut father
to cruise by in his silver ship,
but what he thought was a falling star
was actually his father crashing to earth.

That September morning, it was still dark,
the sheriff, guarded by two muscle-flexing cops,
banged a flashlight on the door.
One blue-boy grabbed my arm
like I was going to leave my kid sleeping upstairs
and run. Where did he think I'd go?
Down a back country road in my nightgown?

Those cartoon symbols for swears
flashed in my head. You set me up,
ex-husband with greed on your mind.
Money hungry at anybody's expense but your own,
wanting cold cash and a bimbo in your bed
bad enough to chuck your kids out in the street
while pressing me under your thumb.

How a Relationship Dies

It doesn't happen in one fell swoop.
It's not the last-straw argument,
the day you walk out and slam the door
wishing you could toss a match behind you.
It's the sand in the shoe that grinds,
the small neglects, disappointments piling up
like mouse droppings in a dark corner.
It's the time you struggle the refrigerator
across the kitchen floor, wrecking your shoulder.
It's the neglected water in the basement that's hell
on your arthritis; it's the day you wake up
and realize you really are alone in this marriage,
the sudden knowing like a comet streaking
the heat burning
everything in its path.

Pink Carnations

It was the lowest day of my life
when I walked into the post office
to find a vase holding three pink carnations
on the edge of the counter
and when the postmaster shouted
his usual cheery *hellohowareya*
I said things would never be good again
and he said, *this is for you*
and handed me the carnations.

Such kindness made me sob
not just for this kindness
but for the all the carnations
the husband who was leaving
never brought home to me.

What If He Wakes?

I.

He holds me in his sleep,
left arm wrapped around my midriff,
his hand under my right breast.

His breath is soft, steady
until I move, then it stops,
starts up again, until I move.

I feel safe under his arm,
my back against him, curled into him.
I feel safe and warm.
I love it.

II.

I feel trapped. I can't sleep this way—

    What if his hand opens, cups my breast?
    What if his fingers stroke my nipple?
    What if he wakes and wants me?

I move just a little,
press myself against him.

He rolls over.
His elbows are sharp.
I hug the pillow for protection.
My breasts have been hurt before.

III.

I love this,
lying here in moonlight watching him,
my fingers tracing his jaw
his chin, his neck,
down his chest.
I draw circles with my forefinger,
curl the chest hairs around my thumb.
He stirs. I stop.

    What if he touches my breast?
    Presses his lips against the nipple
    before I am ready?

IV.

The bed is so warm.
I pull the pillow closer.
He moves his thigh against mine.

    What if he wakes,
    grabs for me
    here in the moonlight?

Close But Not Touching

Eight years together
and we lie here, separated
by a cat, stretched head back
belly exposed, contented
between us, parted by time
and words left unmended.
In sleep we touch briefly
but waken startled and pull back
from what was to what is.
We don't like this
yet make no move toward change,
afraid of refusal, afraid
of what the other might want.
As dawn lights, we smile,
separated, by a cat.

Divorce Settlement

Outside, snow drifts.
Cardinals, the scarlet beauties,
come to feed on seed and suet saved
from a deer felled in fall,
one clear rifle shot singing out,
one sleek stag you dragged home.

The pair perched on the bag of suet
struggles for a strip they can't loose.
First the male, then the female, tugs
one against the other until the fat breaks
and she falls back fluttering,
surprised they've come apart.

In spring you will sell this house—
the roof, rippled and needing repair
will belong to someone else.
The magnolia will blossom.
My red birds returning each winter
like a couple up from Florida
will find me gone.

Working in a Discount Store after the Divorce

Blessings are hard to count—
rock music blaring, cash registers banging,
check-out girls gossiping.
Sun glares through windows so big
I could imagine myself outdoors
if there were no line of customers,
old men in checked shirts,
their insistent puffy fingers
stroking my palm for change,
worn-out women dragging metal carts.

My feet ache. The kids are home
alone after school. We live like transients,
all of us eating in front of the TV,
dressing from baskets of unfolded laundry,
our life fragile as these big glass windows.

Saving the Universe

THEY want me to save the Universe.
Every day in the mail THEY ask my help—
children starving in Bolivia, whales
drowning at sea, seals beaten with clubs.
Don't they know I can't save anyone?
Mother, slipped from this earth
her poor broken heart slowly stopping
while she struggled for breath.
Father, frightened, drowned in his own fluids.
The calico cat ran across the road
before I could swerve or brake.
Some months I can't pay my bills,
bear pain, help my children,
yet the requests keep coming
as if I had a key to the Universe.

Cleaning Her House

While I wash her windows
Billy's mother comes to stare,
the lake gray, sky closing in,
thunderclouds, and rain just spitting.
She tells me about the night he died
how fans whirred inside this cottage.

*Billy was out on the lake
cutting circles with his boat,
it was the way he relaxed after a gig.*

He was twenty-four, talented,
played lead guitar.
His girl had a ring.

*That night there was a noise.
A sort of thunk like a boat
running aground or something
entering water.
I glanced at the mantle clock,
it was midnight.*

*Later, we heard footsteps
and sounds like a turning key.
When death comes fast
you don't realize you've died.*

As I work my cloth into the corners
her hand traces circles in the air.

*His father searched the darkness,
checked the locks.*

His sister lowered her shade;
his brother pacing the beach below
heard nothing but water,
the way it laps over and over
closing in on itself.

Collection Day

It was chance to be standing behind the curtain
when the garbage truck came to a halt.
Watching the man and the young boy who helps him,
suddenly I knew how public garbage is.
In secrecy I shoved old bills and things
under mounds of coffee grounds and orange rinds.
I could see the man in the cab sorting bottles,
hear the chink chink of one against the other.
I almost didn't see the boy in his chubby blue shorts
until he whistled and clapped his hands.
It was almost as if he'd found gold,
the way he chortled and danced around the can
separating bottles from daily necessities.
I didn't mind him collecting the five cents,
it was the crumpled letter never sent,
unfolded and read as if he understood every word.

Birds

I have been painting
and when I lean across the sink
to rinse bristles ragged as the winter bird
squawking beside the empty feeder,
my thoughts turn back to Newtown
where I leaned over a steel sink like this
staring out a picture window
that looked at nothing.
It was 1970, I was between marriages,
three small sons to feed, welfare,
the mortgage two months behind.
I was painting up the house to sell
when who waltzed in but handsome prince
number two. Sexy, steady as a rock,
financially sound. We married
in a finger snap, too quick to know
he'd hate the kids, push each one
from the nest, their necks
nearly snapping in the fall.

After the Party

My guests slam car doors
entering a small space
that excludes me.
I like to imagine their conversations—
how well I looked,
my amazing strength.
In the house, unfinished food,
the good china needing to be washed.

From the porch I count stars.
There is no sound but the sound of moths
against the screen.
Laughter here a moment ago
slips into a memory no one shares.
Words spoken now would shatter
as if words, not silence, could be broken.
I can't get used to absence—
my bed is too wide for one.
Ritual saves me: the locked door,
clean dishes, lights turned out
one by one by one.

IV.

Meeting My Ex at the County Fair

Odd our meeting like this—
a place where pumpkins and cornstalks
are russet and umber with Autumn.
Where people crowd by and the air
smells of beer and fried onions.

Your eyes question mine.
You want to know how it happened,
when he replaced you.
In the seconds a glance takes
I recall your silence.
Like this place ripe with color
I was flesh under taut skin.

If we could talk I would speak of oasis:
how the camel survives without water,
the dry sand and rider's parched mouth,
then, on the horizon, a lake.

At the next stand I buy a fat melon,
two squash, a fist-full of berries
he feeds into my mouth one by one.

Christmas in New York

New York City is all lights,
the tree in Rockefeller Center drawing tourists
like clichéd moths, country people like us
holding each other's mittened hands.
A million miniature lights illuminate angels
half a story high, their gowns, their halos,
the trumpets they lift into air.

On every street corner men roast chestnuts
shoppers jostle packages to the curb.
Cartier is a giant gift tied up in red ribbon,
wood soldiers guarding the doors.
We can't get near Saks,
too many parents and kids
wanting to see the animated window.

Outside the public library on Fifth
black hats sway like smoke stacks.
Two Hassidic Jews discuss a twelfth century Talmud,
their voices rising above buses and the bells
some Salvation Army Santa is ringing.

Traffic is a snarl.
Taxi drivers gesture as if this were any time but Christmas.
Lights blink above the streets,
vendors yell, "get 'em hot!" and the air smells
of burnt chestnuts. A black man plays Silent Night
on a steel drum; four break dancers dance for the crowd
and there's a young man jiving to some rock song
on the boom box he holds in his hand.
A blind man asks assistance, his white stick tapping

the pavement, a drummer's staccato beat.
Beggars rattle their cups, a drunk lies down on the street.
Protestors and sign bearers howl like wolves,
a doomsayer predicts the end.

We hurry to St. Patrick's Cathedral,
the thick oak doors close behind us like a wall.
Everything here is muted; the soft sounds of a wedding
flow from the center altar, flow down from the organ,

Mass bells, the Hail Mary just an undertone. Candles glow.
A priest prays for a couple who in another time,
another place might hide in a church like this,
the noise outside bullets, not backfire.

We put nickels in the prayer box, light candles,
kneel and pray. An old woman wearing worn-out shoes
folds herself down next to us, her hands on the altar rail.
Across the aisle a man sleeps in his army coat.
The tears not cried when my father died come now
and you turn my face away from the man
who reminds me of my father
the way he lay in that mahogany box.

What Hunger Does

At Stop & Shop, seagulls hover
above the parking lot, dive into falling snow
with the frantic urgency of the dying.
Snow deepens. The gulls scream,
beat their wings, fight
for French fries dropped by kids
trekking between McDonald's
and the cement block cinema across the street.

At home, my new husband worries about his father
asleep in his chair, the television playing yesterday's news.
I load groceries into the car, scrape ice crystals
from the windshield. His father dreams
he is fishing with his son on a beach,
gulls hovering above them, like angels.

Rain

This train winds
through a long tunnel.
At home, you wait
in our bed, the soft
tick tick of snow
against the pane.

In the city, rain.
The hem of my jeans
soaks up water.
On Columbus Avenue
I look for a poem.

Five stories up
a window tells
only what it wants
me to know.
When the traffic light
turns red
I miss you.

Far from Home

We sit in a family-run lobster shack
on a pier at the end of a peninsula.
Nobody knows us.
We are relaxed after a winter
of ice and exhausting work that made us bitter.
The sun warms us. The ocean air wafts in.
We are free, far from home.

The scallops on my plate are lightly fried, tender,
the best, I think, that I've ever eaten.
Even the French fries are good.
The coleslaw has some sort of herb
that adds an unfamiliar but delicious flavor.
We are calm. We are on vacation
in Maine. Nobody knows us. We are free.

On the way out of the place we ask directions
back to Bangor. While the owner's grown daughter
carefully writes them out in longhand
on paper torn from an order pad
her mother asks,
Where are you from?
I say Connecticut and she smiles.
I used to live in Kent
a town thirty minutes from our house.
We are in Maine. Nobody knows us.
We are free but for this thin thread.

In Freeport we go to L.L. Bean
to buy much-needed shoes. The salesman—
a tall jaunty man graying at the temples—asks,

Where are you from?
I say Connecticut.
I used to live in Connecticut!
Where?
Newtown, he says, and chills run up my arms.
I grew up in Newtown!
Across from the Hawley Manor. I know the exact house,
    big, brown,
weathered shakes like a Maine shore house,
ivy climbing the white chimney, a half-circle driveway,
a white picket fence.

We are in Maine. Neither of us has been here
in more than thirty years. Long before we knew
each other, long before we expected to be here,
failed marriages behind us, celebrating
our twentieth wedding anniversary
in a lobster shack at the end
of a peninsula where tethered boats
rock in blue water.

Baking Cookies

When I should think of nothing else
but a son home for Christmas
a granddaughter whose almond eyes
watch me roll out cookie dough
memories rise and fill my kitchen
and a woman I once loved comes to mind.
We were friends as close as sisters.
There was nothing I wouldn't do for her.

My granddaughter leans on the table
sprinkles red and green sugar crystals
on top of butter cookies that will melt
in our mouths.
There should be nothing but joy
in this small, blue house,
not this memory—
a friend who leaned into my husband
whispering his name.

As Evening Comes

We sit on the deck an hour before dusk
watching birds fly from tree to feeder and back.

We can't name them all, only the chickadee
finch, titmouse, grosbeak, nuthatch.

It has come to this—
we are quiet observers now

that the children have left the nest.

At the Vet's Office

for Jack

I take our cat to the vet this morning
for the third time in two weeks
and when I say to the cat,
to calm him, or myself,
He hasn't killed you yet,
the vet jokes, *But we'll keep trying!*
and I begin thinking of men,
kind and mean, and how—
unlike this vet I chose
straight off, first visit,
to care for all my pets—
it took me three tries
to find the right man.

The first one I married was a hitter—
open palm, threatening fists,
a knife that promised
to cut my throat before I escaped.

The second one, worse. A handsome man
with no past. I should have known
his clamming up was covering up
what no woman would want to know—
that he lied and cheated and stole and played
head games and made weapons of words
crazy, sick, lazy, liar, leech.

The vet leans over the exam table
gently holding open the cat's eye,

drops in numbing solution, strokes
the cat's white chin, waits patiently
for the eye to freeze
so he can examine the ulcer
on the animal's yellow-green cornea.

The cat's eyes are tearing
and so are mine. The vet says
the procedure isn't hurting the cat
but it hurts me
and I mumble something about not being able

to raise children again, how cat worry
is all I can handle these days,
and he nods.

I know being a vet is not just a job for this man
who would never blow a pheasant apart
with a shotgun, never catch a jackrabbit's foot
in a steel trap, never say killing a deer
is hard work. *You don't know how far
I had to track it before I got a good enough shot,*
the secretive one said.

The cat's eye is numbed and the vet
peers into it with a light, tells me
surgery is necessary to cut out the blight
and tears spring to my eyes again.
The vet blinks and says, *Don't fret,
you will have him back home tonight,*
and I am overwhelmed with gratitude
for the sweet husband who will pick up the cat
and pay the bill without a word.

Poem for a Friend with M.S.

Today we speak of life
knowing death is not far ahead.
We use all the euphemisms
a dying person can stand to hear.
You sound like a poker player—
the hand we are dealt
chips in the ante.
You smile like a train conductor—
life, the great trip
one ticket, one ride.
We agree, life is fatal.

Grief leads me home to my kitchen.
Outside the window, purple dahlias stain the back hill,
hot tea in blue china cups remind me
of the mugs on your shelf.
In six months I watched you slip
from a limp, to a brace, to a wheelchair.
You hid the brace under slacks
but wheelchairs don't lie.
At first, doctors said damaged disks or vertebrae.
Then a glass slipped from your grip.
There was trouble knotting your tie,
trembling, and something sounding like a lisp
by the time they identified M.S.

Your kids are young—
the boy a seven-year-old ball player,
your daughter a sweet ballerina.
Your wife thought marriage was forever.
At night your son tosses a ball to himself.
Your girl rises to her toes, and pirouettes.

Beautiful

My daughter-in-law scurries around
setting out huge platters—
chicken strips, tomatoes, mozzarella,
Prosciutto-wrapped asparagus,
cheese, crackers, dips
and chips for two dozen guests.

It's my granddaughter's birthday.
Aunts, uncles, cousins, friends, four sets of grandparents
gather to celebrate this little girl.

I sit at my daughter-in-law's table,
steam rising like memories from the pasta pot
she lifts from the burner.

Yesterday it was me in my kitchen,
my hands pulling hot dishes from the oven
telling my mother *relax, enjoy*.

My beautiful daughter-in-law keeps smiling
secretly wishes the day done
and I am glad she has no idea
that this crazy, exhausting ritual
will someday end.

Saving For Good

At my age you don't save anything for good.
Now you use that little red purse from Croatia
given to you this Christmas that could be your last.
You take the gold jewelry from the drawer,
clasp the delicate bracelet around your wrist,
hang the filigree earrings on your lobes,
wear the best blouse you own to the grocer's.

You take the good china down from the shelf,
treat the sterling spoons and forks like plastic ware
with daily use. You drink tea from that beautiful cup
you swore you'd pass down to your children,
lay the hand-made lace cloth across the kitchen table,
wear all of it out, use it all up. This
is the time you were saving it for.

AFTERWORD

Jean Sands transformed herself into a different kind of entity after she died on October 8, 2016. Until then she had been a mother, my wife, a journalist, a photographer, a teacher, a poet, a columnist, a friend, and an author—the list could go on. After her death, she evolved into a collective memory, reminiscences of her feminism, her support for fellow writers, her disdain for conservative politicians, her love for mingling with creative people, her search for perfection in all forms of writing.

There was, and is, more to her than all this.

For three years before her health failed, Jean had been writing a second collection of poetry, a book to supplement her debut collection titled *Gandy Dancing* (Antrim House, 2009). She sat at her keyboard or scribbled in notebooks or just stared out at the birds on the feeder waiting for the words to form.

Thus, *Close But Not Touching*, this posthumous collection of poetry, has become yet another entity of Jean Sands. The title poem happens to be the first poem Jean recited for me on our first date in 1987. We were sitting in Friendly's in Torrington, Connecticut, trying to decide if the personal ad she wrote and I answered would lead to anything. "So, you're a poet?" I said. "Could you recite one of your poems for me?"

"I've never been good at memorizing," she said. "But this one's short, so maybe I can remember it."

She looked up at a corner where two walls meet the ceiling, as though she could see the words there. The poem speaks of a former husband, how, when they still shared a bed, there was something between them—they were "separated, by a cat." She said a non-poet friend of hers once remarked, "Wow, I could never write a poem about a cat like that," missing the metaphor.

Lucky for me, I didn't miss it. I think that's why there was a second date, and a third, and nearly three decades of marriage.

And I think that's why the phrase "close but not touching" took on a life of its own in our shared creative world. As a feature writer, I once wrote about an artist whose works were being exhibited in a local gallery, and I showed the story to Jean. She wrote "CBNT" in big red letters across the page.

"What's this?" I said.

"It's close," she said. "But not touching. There's no heart to it, no soul. Who is this artist? I can't feel his presence. He must have said something to reveal why he paints, what drives him, what torments him. Go back and start over."

Writers don't like to hear this kind of criticism, of course. But I needed to hear it, because she was right. And Jean Sands had no problem dishing it out.

What she did have a problem with was human cruelty. "When Mother Stopped Remembering" and "What If?" speak of the importance of remembering past evils so they will not be repeated, speak of how faraway men, women and children could easily be us dying "at the hands of the righteous, / the dictator, the bully."

She had a problem with abuse—physical, sexual, verbal, emotional—and how, as in "The Peach Farmer's Daughter," it can wound a person for life.

But she rejoiced in family, how—as in "Turn That Goddamn Thing Down"—they can drive you nuts until they're gone and you yearn for the things that drove you nuts.

And she rejoiced in the rare moments of the kindnesses of strangers, as in the jovial postmaster's gift of "Pink Carnations" when she needed to feel loved.

Each one of these poems is a version of Jean Sands, an essence of Jean Sands' words gathered into this new embodiment that allow her to live and breathe again. Because this book exists in the world, her poems will keep her close to me—and, I hope, to you.

Jack Sheedy

About the Author

Jean Sands is the author of the poetry collection *Gandy Dancing* (Antrim House, 2009), which won a 2014 Eric Hoffer Legacy Award and was a finalist for that year's Eric Hoffer First Horizon Award and the Eric Hoffer Montaigne Medal. Her poetry has been published in literary journals, anthologized, and nominated for a Pushcart Prize. She also served as a journalist, reviewer, columnist and correspondent whose interviews, essays, and feature articles appeared in regional and national publications as well as online. Jean served as a poet in the schools and taught poetry and creative writing to adults throughout northwest Connecticut for over twenty years. She was preparing the present collection for publication when she died in 2016.

This book is set in Garamond Premier Pro, which originated in 1988 when type-designer Robert Slimbach visited the Plantin-Moretus Museum in Antwerp, Belgium, to study its collection of Claude Garamond's metal punches and typefaces. During the mid-fifteen hundreds, Garamond—a Parisian punch-cutter—produced a refined array of book types that combined an unprecedented degree of balance and elegance, for centuries standing as the pinnacle of beauty and practicality in type-founding. Slimbach has created an entirely new interpretation based on Garamond's designs and on compatible italics cut by Robert Granjon, Garamond's contemporary.

To order additional copies of this book
or other Antrim House titles, contact the publisher at

Antrim House
21 Goodrich Rd., Simsbury, CT 06070
860.217.0023, AntrimHouse@comcast.net
or the house website (www.AntrimHouseBooks.com).

•

On the house website
in addition to information on books
you will find sample poems, upcoming events,
and a "seminar room" featuring supplemental biography,
notes, images, poems, reviews, and
writing suggestions.

www.ingramcontent.com/pod-product-compliance
Lightning Source LLC
Chambersburg PA
CBHW040417100526
44588CB00022B/2853